EVERY CHILD IS GIFTED
Written by Joy Gorham Hervey
Illustrated by Verna Mae Cann

Every Child is Gifted

By Joy Gorham Hervey
© Copyright 2012 Joy Gorham Hervey. All rights reserved.

No portion of this book may be reproduced by any means, electronic or mechanical, including photocopying, recording, or by any information storage retrieval system, without permission of the copyright's owner, except for the inclusion of brief quotations for a review.

ISBN: 978-1-935986-48-5

Lynchburg, VA

www.liberty.edu/LibertyUniversityPress

Author's Dedication
To my mom and dad, James and Linda Gorham, whose heroic cultivation of their own children's giftedness has always been matched by their loving, sacrificial commitment to providing opportunities for other people's children. Thank you for being my example.

Illustrator's Dedication
All honor to God, who has made all these things possible.

Some children live in mansions next to sparkling waterfalls

And some live in adobe huts with grass roofs and warm walls.

No matter what your lot in life, the hands that made us all

Have shaped us with a purpose that awaits His gentle call.

Every child is gifted.
Every child can learn.
Within the poor and homeless child,
A precious gift may churn.

With love and care and patience, it will blossom, bloom, and grow;
Like a flower seeking sunlight, hidden talent soon will show.

Some grownups are forever sorting: smart kids here and slow ones there;
The ones called gifted get big smiles, while others, silent, sit and stare.

They hope and dream and try again,
But harsh words dim the light within;
Their brilliance sputters like a flame
That flickers in the unjust wind.

All the while, the gifts within them
Shout out to be seen;
He loves big words, she brings home pets,
Another's thumb is green.

This child has a flair for fashion; that one has a painter's eye.
The nurse, chef, poet, handyman -
They all showed signs when just knee-high.

Every child is gifted, yes, every child can learn;
That rule is universal, no matter where you turn.
Kofi opens clock and toaster, and then puts them back together;

Mei-Ling reads from dusk to dawn, while José runs despite the weather.

When Lisa plays school,
She is always the teacher.

When Manny's in church,
His amens spark the preacher.

Young Abe is courageous,
A natural guide.

Trinh's sweet melodies fill her parents with pride.

A wheelchair or a stutter may obscure your walk or talk;

Folks may comment on your beauty or may tease and taunt and gawk.

But the gift that burns within you
Will, one day, be seen by all;
Seeds you plant by helping others
Will take root and grow up tall.

Like eagles spread their wings to fly, get ready, take your turn,

For you, my child, are gifted, and you, my child, can learn.

EVERY CHILD IS GIFTED
by Joy Gorham Hervey

Some children live in mansions
Next to sparkling waterfalls
And some live in adobe huts
With grass roofs and warm walls.

No matter what your lot in life,
The hands that made us all
Have shaped us with a purpose
That awaits His gentle call.

Every child is gifted.
Every child can learn.
Within the poor and homeless child,
A precious gift may churn.

With love and care and patience,
It will blossom, bloom, and grow;
Like a flower seeking sunlight,
Hidden talent soon will show.

Some grownups are forever sorting:
Smart kids here and slow ones there;
The ones called gifted get big smiles,
While others, silent, sit and stare.

They hope and dream and try again,
But harsh words dim the light within;
Their brilliance sputters like a flame
That flickers in the unjust wind.

All the while, the gifts within them
Shout out to be seen;
He loves big words, she brings home pets,
Another's thumb is green.

This child has a flair for fashion;
That one has a painter's eye.
The nurse, chef, poet, handyman -
They all showed signs when just knee-high.

Every child is gifted,
Yes, every child can learn;
That rule is universal,
No matter where you turn.

Kofi opens clock and toaster,
Then he puts them back together;
Mei-Ling reads from dusk to dawn,
While José runs despite the weather.

When Lisa plays school,
She is always the teacher.
When Manny's in church,
His amens spark the preacher.

Young Abe is courageous,
A natural guide.
Trinh's sweet melodies
Fill her parents with pride.

A wheelchair or a stutter may
Obscure your walk or talk;
Folks may comment on your beauty
Or may tease and taunt and gawk.

But the gift that burns within you
Will, one day, be seen by all;
Seeds you plant by helping others
Will take root and grow up tall.

Like eagles spread their wings to fly,
Get ready, take your turn;
For you, my child, are gifted,
And you, my child, can learn.

About the Author

Joy Gorham Hervey was born and raised in Baltimore, Maryland. As a child, she loved to read and write. "I remember losing myself in books," she said. Fortunately, her parents gave her many opportunities to do so and instilled in her a passion to provide similar opportunities to others. "I love to see children get excited about reading."

Joy skipped her senior year of high school and attended Harvard University, where she met her husband, Eurmon. Following in her mother's footsteps, Joy pursued her calling as an educator, working as a teacher, principal, consultant, professor, and leader of community programs. She has earned a master's degree from the Harvard Graduate School of Education and a doctorate from Columbia Teachers College.

While completing her dissertation research in Ghana, Joy met a young man pursuing engineering who talked about how he spent his childhood taking things apart and putting them back together. He makes an appearance in this book, along with the author's children, Emmanuel and Trinity, two incredibly talented and loving kids who inspire her daily. Joy lives with her family in Jacksonville, Florida. In addition to reading and writing, she enjoys music and bargain-hunting.

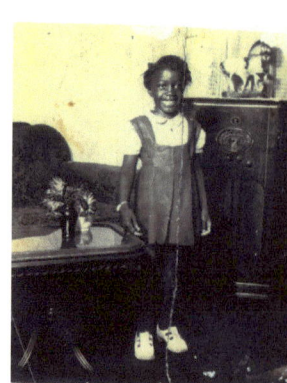

About the Illustrator

Verna Mae Cann, the author's grandmother, is "so tickled" to have this opportunity to fulfill her lifelong dream of illustrating children's books. Verna spent her childhood years in Durham, North Carolina, then moved to Baltimore, Maryland, as a young woman. There, she attempted to enroll in art school to study illustration but was turned away because of segregation. Still, she developed her natural artistic talents in drawing, painting, quiltmaking, pottery, sculpting, woodworking, creative writing, sign and mural design, song writing, singing, dramatic arts, and videography. Wherever she goes, Verna is known as the "artist in residence," always creating art and teaching others to do the same. Verna obtained her college degree as an adult and went on to have a successful twenty-year career as a social worker. She has been blessed with two children, three grandchildren, and four great-grandchildren (and counting). Verna lives in Parkton, Maryland with her family.

Also by the Author

DREAMPOWER:
Using Life Lessons, Research-Based Practices, and the Psychology of Motivation to Win in Education
Paperback, 235 pages, $19.95 plus shipping & handling

This resource for educators breaks new ground by combining positive psychology with heart-warming stories. Authors Little and Hervey support research findings in human motivation with real-life experiences and cues from best educational practices. They highlight what works to motivate today's students, communicate and develop partnerships with parents, and address the necessity of self-mastery. Along the way, the duo highlights trend-setting educators who are enlisting new approaches to motivation and pointing a bold way forward. **DREAMPOWER,** a provocative and readable desktop companion, is guaranteed to challenge every educator to rethink and improve the ways in which schools motivate students, teachers, and parents.

Visit www.genesisconsultinggroupllc.com to order your copy today!

www.ingramcontent.com/pod-product-compliance
Lightning Source LLC
Chambersburg PA
CBHW041934160426
42813CB00103B/2941